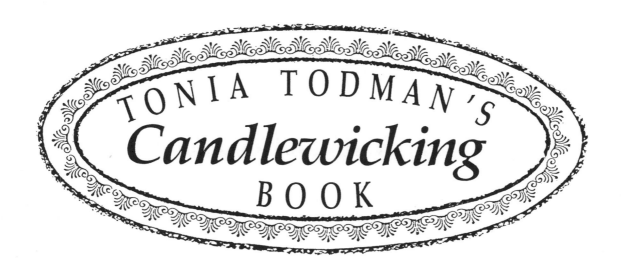

TONIA TODMAN'S
Candlewicking
BOOK

SALLY MILNER PUBLISHING

First published in 1993 by
Sally Milner Publishing Pty Ltd
558 Darling Street
Rozelle NSW 2039 Australia

Reprinted 1993

© Todman Services Pty Ltd, 1993

Design and typesetting by Gatya Kelly, Doric Order
Photography by Andrew Elton
Illustrations and patterns by Lesley Griffith
Printed in Australia by Impact Printing, Melbourne

National Library of Australia
Cataloguing-in-Publication data:

Tonia, Todman
    Tonia Todman's candlewicking book.

    ISBN 1 86351 104 0.

    1.Candlewicking (Embroidery) — Patterns. I. Title.
    II. Title: Candlewicking book. (Series : Milner craft series).

746.44041

Contents

The author wishes to acknowledge the designs of Sue Millard
which have been reproduced on some of the pages in this book.

Introduction

I have long been fascinated by the origins of candlewicking embroidery. The story is a romantic one of American pioneer women creating embroideries as they crossed the prairies with their families, driving their covered wagons towards their new life in some far-off, unknown place. The story has probably been embellished by the imaginings of successive generations — but it's a happy story and I'd like to share it with you.

It seems that while the long journey across America was fraught with dangers — angry Indians, the inhospitable terrain, lack of food and medical supplies to name only a few — there were quiet moments around the camp fires at night that made the men and women's thoughts turn to more homely pastimes.

The men repaired the wagons and tended the horses, and then probably relaxed by indulging in whittling — the age-old craft of carving small objects from wood. Needlecrafts were second nature to women of this era. These pioneer women founded a new form of embroidery, based only on those materials they had to hand, and shaped by the difficult conditions in which they worked.

The wagons were covered with a canopy of firm, canvas-like, cream cotton fabric, and each one was equipped with an extra length of the fabric to be used for patching the canopy. The only plentiful supply of 'thread' was the wicking from candles. This happened to be of cotton, too, and was of much the same colour as the canopy fabric. It was thick but smooth, but was entirely different from the silk or other cotton threads traditionally used in fine embroidery. The only light women had to work by came from candles or a fire, so precise and intricate embroidery was out of the question. The thick thread, the poor illumination and the coarse fabric combined to produce an embroidery made mainly of textured knots — either the Colonial or the French knot. These knots could be 'felt' as much as seen under candlelight, and the thickness of the wicking gave the work a texture that easily disguised inaccuracies. The finished work was later washed in a stream, then draped across nearby bushes or a wagon's canopy to dry; ironing was simply not an option. Quilts, bed linen and clothing were all trimmed with candle-wicking embroidery and the crumpled, textured look remains today as the hallmark of this traditional stitch.

I believe much of today's candlewicking embroidery has become too refined with the addition of many other stitches and the use of less rustic threads. Many pieces have lost their character because the actual knotting content is so 'diluted'. To define embroidery as true candlewicking, I feel the design should show an emphasis on the use of knotting stitches and cream threads, with only a few other traditional, textured stitches employed for variety.

Candlewicking embroidery is ideal for the beginner. When you recall its origins and the conditions under which it was first stitched, you can easily understand how informal it can be. It is easy to learn the basic knots, and the other stitches used to complement them are old favourites, beloved by embroiderers for generations.

A quilt motif. The dots are all knots and the centre rails could either be stem stitch, or filled with satin stitch

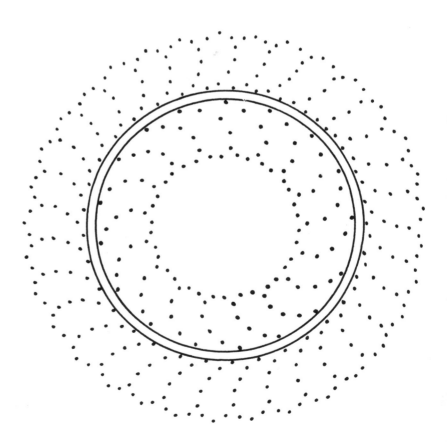

Threads and fabrics used in candlewicking

Yesterday and today

Synthetic fabrics as we know them today were probably beyond the imaginings of the original candlewickers. The fabrics of their era were certainly loomed mechanically, but they were always made from natural fibres. Cotton was the most common one in America, even though it was all imported in the early days. These fabrics were woven for strictly utilitarian household purposes, with no thought to evenness of weave or precision of thread thickness — and certainly not with an embroiderer's needs in mind. I imagine the average cotton weaver would have been most surprised to see the plain, unpretentious fabric embellished with pretty embroidery!

While the raw cotton was cleansed and combed prior to spinning and weaving, very often seeds were allowed to remain in the finished fabric, giving it a spotted, or peppered, appearance. The resulting fabrics were very similar to the inexpensive, unbleached varieties of calicos that come today from India and China — sometimes thick and stiff like canvas, and sometimes thin and sheer like muslin. It was with this thick, canvas-like fabric that wagon canopies were covered, and it's this that the first candlewickers used as a base for their embroidery.

The fabric was coarse and stiff to work with, softening only when washed after the embroidery was completed. This washing process has a fascinating purpose. Apart from the obvious need to cleanse the finished item (it had, after all, been unavoidably worked in difficult, sometimes dirty situations), there was a definite need to shrink the fabric. One of the most charming complementary stitches used with the traditional knots was known as

tufting. These stitches were worked in loops and later clipped to resemble tufted carpet sections. When the fabric shrank, these tufted sections were held tightly into the weave of the material and were prevented from working loose.

History has shown examples of candlewicking done only on cotton or linen fabrics, but I know it is also charming on wool and silk fabrics of various weights and textures. These other applications of candlewicking are obviously modern, the fabrics themselves helping to make the embroidery appear more contemporary.

Candlewicking (the cotton wick embedded in candles from which the embroidery takes its name) is a textured cotton thread twisted together to form a strong, fine cord. Manufacturers of embroidery threads soon realised that today's sewers would appreciate a candlewicking embroidery thread that replicated the texture, strength and colour of the original candlewicking, and set about making just that. The threads available today for embroidery in general are varied, and most can be used for candlewicking. However, for a true effect, you should seek out cards or balls of modern candlewicking embroidery thread — it should be unbleached, strong and fairly inexpensive. It is quite distinguishable from other threads, is not divided into separate strands to be used, and will usually be labelled 'candlewicking thread'. This thread also tends to swell slightly and fluff up after washing, making for tighter knots. An economical and effective substitute can be cream crochet thread. This is woven in a similar way to traditional candlewicking thread and is a comparable, authentic colour. A disadvantage is that it is usually lustrous whereas the traditional thread is not.

When candlewicking strays from the traditional image of cream threads on cream fabric, some careful thought needs to be given to the combination of threads and fabric so that the resulting piece doesn't become characterless. I tend to prefer embroidering wool fabric with wool yarn. Embroidering knots demands a smooth thread, so your wool yarn must be smooth and untextured. Because of this, homespuns may be out of the question. Mohairs and other fluffy yarns may be suitable, but the knots would need to be quite large in order to be seen through the fluff. Tapestry yarns are ideal because they are super-strong, usually available in a wonderful colour range and are just the right thickness to fit a medium-sized crewel-eyed needle.

Using silk fabric as a base results in a more lustrous, feminine piece that is suitable for lingerie, baby wear or, perhaps, an elegant silk cushion. Silk ribbon is available now in a multitude of colours, thanks to the surge in interest in Heirloom sewing. This ribbon is 3 mm ($1/8$") wide and is incredibly soft and glossy; it sews beautifully into knots. Silk ribbon knots can look lovely too, on a fine, wool flannel fabric, making this ribbon ideal for embellishing such things as a baby's blanket.

Traditional stranded embroidery thread is also an effective medium with which to work. Again, it is lustrous, smooth and easy to use, and the colour range is extensive. There are several alternative threads within the 'embroidery thread' category and I suggest you try them all. Some are thicker, others are more glossy than traditional stranded thread. Yet more are made of pure silk and can be used for very fine work. When choosing yarns, bear in mind that the thicker the yarn or number of threads you use, the larger your knots will be.

Quilt motif. These solid lines can be stem stitch or rows of knots. Small amounts of colour, or a single colour, would provide added interest. For example, you could pick out the centre of the heart, the birds' tails, the flowers and the ribbons coming from the birds, in a colour

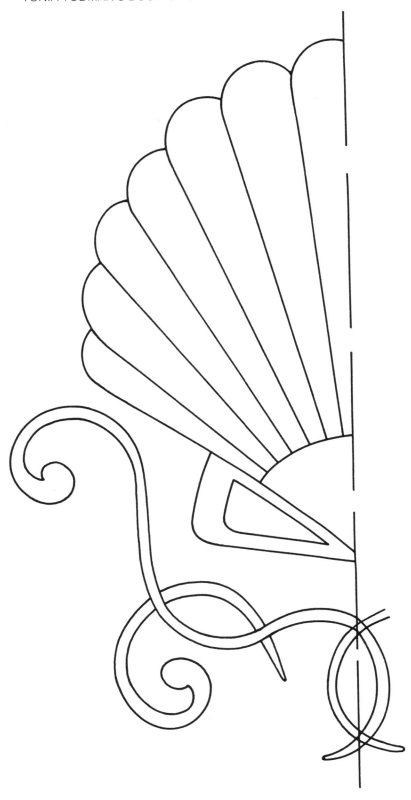

Quilt motifs. Rows of knots, or stem stitch, are used here. Thicker threads will add texture in places and you could try adding colour in small amounts. Duplicate the identical side of the designs before stitching

Materials used in candlewicking

Fabrics

Traditional fabrics were of the cotton canvas variety, unwashed at the time of embroidering. Today we can use lighter and softer varieties of unbleached and unwashed calico or muslin. Or, we can substitute similar, more refined cotton fabrics. Wools (providing they are closely woven) and silks that are not too textured can also be effective bases for candlewicking. Fabrics must be closely woven because of the knotted stitches used. Knotted stitches sit on top of the fabric, with the thread being pulled down through it to complete the stitch. If the fabric is too open, that final action will pull both thread and knot down through the fabric to the other side, thus ruining the stitch.

Threads

Traditional candlewicking thread — which may be difficult to find at times — crochet cotton, Coton à broder and Perle (both DMC embroidery threads), stranded embroidery thread, silk ribbon and wool or cotton tapestry yarn are all suitable. Always remember that the size of your yarn is relative to the completed knot — the fewer strands of thread you use, the smaller your knot.

Needles

Any crewel-eye needle that is the appropriate size for the thread you are using is suitable. Do not use a needle with a blunt point, such as a tapestry needle, on closely woven fabrics.

8

Embroidery hoop

All work must be done while using an embroidery hoop. To make your embroidery a more pleasant task, note the changes I suggest you make to a standard embroidery hoop, shown in the illustration. You will need to purchase two hoops of the same size, discarding the outer ring of one hoop. By having the space fixed between the hoops you have constant access to both sides of the work, without having to continually lift and lower it. The hoops sit neatly on your lap, or a table top, and are not heavy. The arrangement of the hoops is very well suited to the candlewicking embroidery process, and I've found that it certainly makes stitching a lot faster. If you are embroidering a pattern piece that's only marginally bigger than the dimensions of your hoop, embroider the complete design first, then cut out the piece from the fabric.

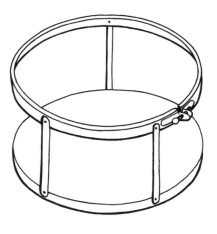

Embroidery hoop

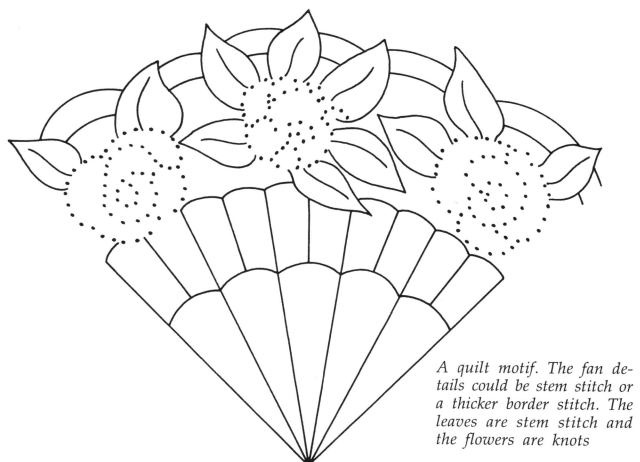

A quilt motif. The fan details could be stem stitch or a thicker border stitch. The leaves are stem stitch and the flowers are knots

Transfer pencil, or dressmaker's carbon

Ideally, you should use some form of washable pen or transfer pencil to draw your embroidery design onto your fabric. If these are not available, use dressmaker's carbon paper to leave an imprint, or simply draw the design onto the fabric using a soft, well-sharpened lead pencil. After the embroidery is complete, rub away any visible lead pencil with an eraser; the remainer should come away with the first washing. Often a window can be used as a 'light box', allowing you to trace off a design with the aid of the natural light illuminating the pattern. To work this way, hold the design behind the fabric and press them both against the window while drawing. See the note later in the introduction of the Two Heirloom Quilt projects (page 36) for more ideas about transferring a design.

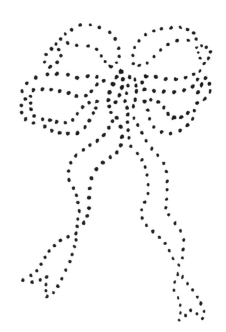

Creative thoughts on where to use candlewicking embroidery

Traditional items for embroidery

Museum pieces show us that household linen was the first possession that pioneer women embellished. Sheet fold-backs, pillowcase edges and quilts have all remained for us to wonder over and admire. Table linen, short curtain frills, samplers, cushion covers and doilies were all enthusiastically embroidered with candlewicking; all are still wonderfully appropriate for embroidery today. Bed-spreads were beautifully candlewicked, and we can still see extensive areas of tufting stitch on some surviving bedspreads.

Quilts were quite commonplace, candlewicking lending itself very well to quilts of several classifications:

- Whole fabric quilts, where there is no traditional piecing of fabric shapes on the quilt top. Instead, the fabric is intricately embroidered as one whole piece.

- Pieced quilts, where simple squares, or more complex shapes, are pieced together across the quilt top. More often than not, each square is embroidered with a different pattern.

- Crazy quilts, where fabric scraps of any size and shape are joined, with the joined edges disguised by

11

rows of embroidery. The fabric shapes are then individually embroidered, frequently with candlewicking knots and complementary stitches.

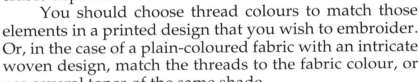

Embroidering printed fabric

Because the knots used in candlewicking have a very noticeable texture, especially when clustered together, they can be used to 're-embroider' printed fabric to great effect. For example, imagine a glossy, cotton chintz fabric with an all-over print of pretty bunches of roses surrounded by smaller field flowers. The centre of the roses, the veins of the leaves and the underneath of the rose petals could be embroidered, and the field flowers filled in where possible. Or, you could re-embroider a tribal or batik print, or give greater interest to a jacquard silk or linen damask pattern by regularly embroidering some part of the woven-in fabric pattern. The effect of this work is to soften the pattern of the fabric, and to give it considerable depth and surface texture.

You should choose thread colours to match those elements in a printed design that you wish to embroider. Or, in the case of a plain-coloured fabric with an intricate woven design, match the threads to the fabric colour, or use several tones of the same shade.

Samplers

A framed sampler is a charming heirloom and can be as simple or complex as you wish. You could simply reproduce traditional patchwork motifs in miniature to look like a small, framed quilt worked only in simple border stitches and knots. Or, it could look just like a traditional student's sampler that features every embroidery technique associated with candlewicking, and a variety of motifs, letters and numbers. The advantage of a sampler is that it is small, portable and, therefore, able to be embroidered anywhere. They're usually quick to finish, too. Good, encouraging thoughts for a novice candlewicker, I feel!

When working a sampler, always allow a border of blank fabric of at least 3 cm ($1^1/_4$ ") around the edge of the outermost embroidery which will remain showing in the framed sampler, plus extra beyond this to make working with your hoop easy. I also suggest that you always wrap the edges of your embroidery fabric with masking tape, or overcast them by hand or machine to prevent fraying during the embroidery process.

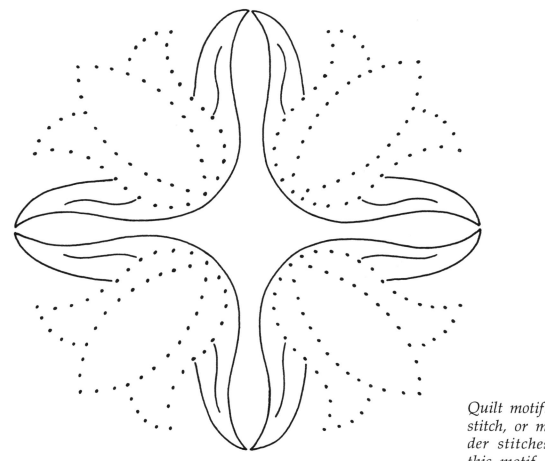

Quilt motif. The use of stem stitch, or more textured border stitches, is effective in this motif.

How to block and frame your sampler

Choose a frame that is at least 3 cm ($1^1/_4$") smaller all round than the size of your sampler. To frame your sampler when you've finished embroidering, place the completed work right side down onto a fluffy towel placed on an ironing board. Pin the sampler's edges onto the ironing board by pushing the pins through the sampler into the board, stretching the sampler's edges slightly and adjusting them to be straight and parallel. When all edges are taut and straight, smoothly press the back of the work with a steam iron. You might like to spray the back lightly with a mist of water to help the smoothing process. Allow the sampler to dry in the blocked position and only remove it when it is completely cool.

Cut a piece of strong cardboard to be 3 mm ($1/_8$") smaller all round than the opening at the back of your frame. Find the centre of the cardboard and the centre of the sampler and pin the sampler to the cardboard, matching these points. Making sure the embroidery is sitting straight, fold the upper and lower edges to the back of the cardboard and hold them there temporarily with adhesive or masking tape. Thread a needle with a long, double length of strong sewing thread. Pass the needle through the edge of the sampler top. Then pass it through the edge of the sampler bottom. Continue to stitch from one edge to the other pulling the thread firmly until the top and bottom are evenly laced together. Your stitches should be about 1.5 cm ($1/_2$") apart. Fasten off the thread securely. Repeat this process with the sampler's side edges.

If you are using glass to protect your sampler (and I suggest you do) insert this in the frame now, then insert the sampler. Tack in any necessary nails to the frame edge to keep the sampler and glass secure. Cover the back of the sampler with a sheet of firm cardboard, taping its edges down with masking tape or a similar adhesive tape. Fasten any hooks and wire needed to hang the sampler.

Traditional candlewicking motifs

Traditional candlewicking motifs were very simple. The women used folk motifs that were a familiar part of their European heritage — motifs we can still see used extensively in examples of painted folk art. Hearts, roses, birds, lace borders, posies, animals, houses and figures were all drawn freehand onto the fabric and then embroidered.

Most old examples of candlewicking show that the knots were usually used to outline a motif, rather than filling it in. The overall effect of this technique is one of lightness. And because the motifs were rarely symmetrical or even mathematically accurate in their shapes, the work was imbued with a simple charm. Often messages were written on old pieces, the letters and numbers later being filled in with tiny rows of knots.

A great deal of sentiment often went into designing a candlewicked piece. Motifs bearing no connection to each other may appear side by side, prompted no doubt by the embroiderer's memories, and her efforts to catch them forever in embroidery. In some ways, early embroideries were similar to today's photo albums. Births, deaths and marriages were recorded in the embroidered quilts and samplers, while cushions may capture a favoured pet, house or garden. Children's growing years and achievements were noted in embroideries also.

The embroidery stitches

The stitches used in candlewicking are not extensive, and are simple to make. Keep in mind that they were meant to be 'felt' — that is, their surface texture was important — and the original overall effect of the embroidery was subtle and informal, rather than bold and near to perfect in its execution.

The Knots

There are basically only two knots — the French knot, and the Colonial knot. Both are simple, differing only in the method of winding the thread around the needle. Naturally, the finished profile of your knot will depend on the number of threads you have through your needle, or the thickness of the single strand. Finding your ideal size is a matter for experimentation. You will note that much of the embroidery shown in this book features knots of various sizes. These are achieved by using fewer or more strands, or thicker or thinner thread, or combining threads of different textures and glossiness.

Candlewicking experts will often say they prefer to use the Colonial knot, and I tend to agree. I believe it to be neater and think it sits better when completed. However, you should use whichever you prefer. Several of the stitches are 'outline' stitches, used for stems, borders, words and similar areas which require emphasising. These outline stitches are sometimes interchangeable, so experiment and substitute your preferred stitch if you wish.

Left-handed embroiderers will find the illustrations easier to understand if they first prop the book in front of a mirror and follow the reflected images.

French Knot

- Bring your needle up through the fabric. Wind the thread around the needle twice. *(Photo Step 1)* Reinsert the tip of the needle into the fabric *(Photo*

16

Step 2). While holding the remainder of your thread taut with one hand, take the needle through the fabric, thus taking the thread down through the wound thread or 'knot'.

- I like to hold the remaining thread taut until only a little remains to be taken through the knot, then move that hand to have the fingers underneath the work and the thumb on top of the knot, making sure the winding does not spring undone.

- Continue to pull the thread through to the back firmly until the knot sits well. The wound thread has been secured and it is this which will form a knot on the fabric surface. Bring the needle back up through your work for the next knot. Some embroiderers prefer to only wind their thread around the needle once, others three times. Naturally, the more winds the larger your knot. I suggest you experiment and decide which number you prefer to work with.

Colonial Knot

- Bring your needle through the fabric. Holding the thread in your left hand, and holding the needle firmly with your right hand, wind the thread, as shown, around the needle forming a looped figure of 8. *(Photo Steps 1 & 2)* Pull the thread with your left hand, gently tightening the loops around the needle, at the same time inserting the tip of the needle back into the fabric. *(Photo Step 3)*

- As with the French Knot, pull the needle through the wound thread down into the fabric, at the same time releasing the thread with your left hand and moving your hand across to hold the knot firmly between your thumb and fingers. I do not suggest you wind more than one figure of 8 around your needle; instead, use thicker thread if a bulkier knot is required.

17

Stem Stitch

- This is one of the simplest stitches to make. It produces a neat, raised line which has a rather rope-like appearance. It is best if stitched with small, even stitches. You will naturally stitch back towards you, although your finished work stretches away from you.

- Bring the needle out at A, down through the fabric at B and out at C. Repeat this as often as needed, keeping the working thread to the left of the needle. While you're stitching in virtually a straight line, your stitches will take on a slightly diagonal appearance.

Stem Stitch

Chain Stitch

- This stitch is ideal for following curved borders or outlines, and can be used extensively for filling spaces.

- Bring your needle up through the fabric, place the needle back in the fabric next to where it emerged and take a short stitch, keeping the thread under the tip of the needle. Pull the needle through making your first chain.

- Repeat this process taking short, even stitches to build your length of chain stitch. Do not pull your thread too tightly; this will distort the shape of your chains. Rather you should aim to have an even tension throughout, allowing the chains to sit snugly but evenly on top of the fabric.

- The thickness of chain stitch can sometimes overpower clusters of knots and other parts of the overall embroidery. This would probably be more of a problem if you wanted to use chain stitch for a stem or some other connecting line. Consider the thickness of the chain stitch in comparison to the parts that branch off it and be sure it is all in proportion. Stem stitch, or back stitch, are the finest stitches.

Chain Stitch

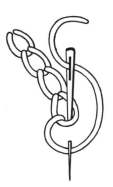

Back Stitch

- Before sewing machines, this was the strong stitch which held garments together. It still has that asset of strength, but can also be effective as a subtle border or outline stitch. It is best described as a line of small, evenly spaced stitches worked from right to left — or towards you if it is more comfortable that way.

- Bring the needle out at point A. Insert the needle to the right of point A at B, bringing it out at C on the left of A. Return the needle down through A and repeat these steps as often as necessary. On the back of your work you will have overlapped stitches.

Back Stitch

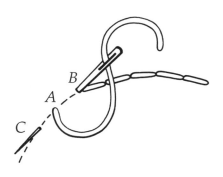

Blanket Stitch

- Just as the name implies, this traditional stitch was used to bind the edges of thickly woven wool blankets. It was usually worked in matching wool or a heavy cotton yarn, and the stitch still looks good when made with a thick yarn of any description. It can also look effective as a border, especially when the stitches are close together. Naturally, this close-up stitching is an ideal edge to hand-appliquéd pieces. It is not a stitch you would traditionally find accompanying candlewicked pieces, except when used as an edging. The stitch is worked from left to right.

- To start a row of stitching, take a stitch on the wrong side of the fabric that catches threads just sufficient to hold it, yet does not show through onto the right side. Bring your needle to the right side of the fabric.

- Take your needle up to the depth of stitch required and take it through to the wrong side at point A, bringing it out at point B with the thread under the needle. Pull the thread firmly, but not so tightly that you distort or pucker the fabric.

- Continue to work in the same way, keeping the thread under the needle, until sufficient stitches have been made.

Blanket Stitch

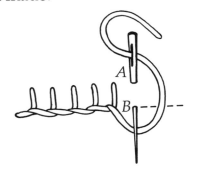

Couching Stitch

- Couching stitch has endured as a favourite from the time of the earliest-known embroideries. One of the most effective border stitches, it is flexible and, therefore useful for curves and tight corners. It is very simple to stitch.

- Lay down a thick thread following a design line. Thread a needle with a thinner thread and bring it up through the design line just below the flat thread.

- Take stitches at even intervals over the flat thread to hold it in place. Do take care to space your stitches about 3 mm ($^1/_8$") to 6 mm ($^1/_4$") apart. If they are too close, they spoil the couched effect. If they are too spacious the flat thread distorts as it is not being held sufficiently well on the design line.

Couching Stitch

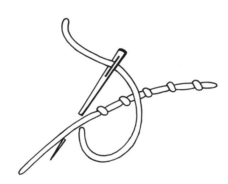

Scroll Stitch

- This very simple border stitch could be used in the same situations you may have considered for couching stitch. As you are working with one thread only it will be even simpler than couching. The stitch has a knotted appearance, and works very well with candlewicking. I suggest you try to use a thicker thread than usual so that the stitch has an interesting surface texture. You can place your stitches quite close together to form a row of scrolled knots, or space them further apart, but still evenly spaced, for another interesting effect.

- To start, bring the stitch through from the back of the fabric. With the thread above and behind the needle, scoop a small, angled stitch through the fabric from A to B, with the thread coming around anti-clockwise to be under the tip of the emerging needle.

- Pull your threads gently but firmly, being sure the surface knots sit evenly.

- Continue to take evenly spaced stitches until a sufficient amount is worked.

Scroll Stitch

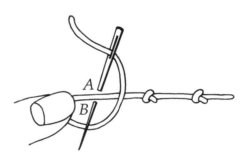

Quilt motif. These solid lines can be stem stitch or rows of knots. Small amounts of colour, or a single colour, would provide added interest. For example, you could pick out the centre of the heart, the birds' tails, the flowers and the ribbons coming from the birds, in a colour

A quilt motif. The basket detail is stem stitch and the flowers are a combination of knots, satin stitch, lazy-daisy stitch and stem stitch. The bow outline could be satin stitch or stem stitch

Candlewicking projects

Lined Embroidery Basket

Threads to match the colours in the rose-patterned chintz lining have been used to embroider the basket's padded, lift-up flaps. This is a simple, time-honoured style of work basket. I felt the two flap tops were just right to feature candlewick embroidery that echoed the pretty fabric. I think this basket would attract an embroiderer of any age and would be especially inspiring to any young lady embarking on her first needlework projects. The method of making the basket will be common to a basket of any size of this style. Your fabric requirements will vary, but quantities will be easy to estimate because you will need to make paper patterns of each section of the basket before you can start.

Tip: A basket with a handle, but without lift-up flaps, can still be used for this project. Make flaps to fit by cutting them from strong cardboard, then cover them in the same way as the cane flaps.

Please read measuring, pattern making and cutting instructions before purchasing fabrics and materials. Use your machine's zipper foot for making and applying bias piping, and overcast all exposed raw edges.

MATERIALS

* Cane basket with flaps for opening that has a distinctly flat base. It should be sprayed with clear gloss lacquer or paint, if desired

25

- Paper for pattern making, such as brown paper, white butcher's paper or strong tissue paper. Do not use newspaper because the print sometimes rubs off on fabric

- Medium-thickness quilter's batting for flaps and inner base lining

- Printed fabric for double-thickness lining

- Fabric to be embroidered for flap tops. I suggest calico or quilter's muslin or homespun

- Piping cord, or ready-made piping in a colour to match the lining fabric

- Sewing thread

- Embroidery threads to match the lining fabric

METHOD FOR PATTERN MAKING

- Remove the flaps from the basket. This may involve cutting away thin ties of cane that secure them to the central bar across the basket. The flaps are later fastened back onto the basket with fabric ties.

- Make a pattern of the flaps by pressing a piece of paper over them and running your finger nail around the outside edge. This indentation can then be used as a cutting guide, after you have added a 1 cm ($^3/_8$") seam allowance.

- Make a pattern of the inner basket base using your finger nail again to make the marks.

- Measure around the outer circumference of the lip of the basket. Then, measure the depth from the inside of the lip down to the edge of the inner basket base. Note these measurements. Decide how far down the outside of the basket you wish your lining to fall.

- Cut out and duplicate a pattern which measures half the length of the circumference plus 8 cms (3") for ease, and has a depth equal to where the lining will start on the outside of the basket, then over the lip down inside to meet the base. Add 1 cm ($^3/_8$") seams to all pattern pieces. This pattern will provide the basket wall lining pieces, and will be gathered around the edge of the base piece, with the splits between the two wall pieces allowing for the handle bases.

- Crease the base piece in half and mark the half-way points at the edges. Pin the pattern lining pieces in small pleats around the base, stopping and starting at the half-way crease. This crease should pass across the base under the line of the handle. The base should fit flat across the bottom of the basket, and the lining pieces should travel up the walls of the basket, over the lip and down the outside to the desired depth. You will soon see where you need to make adjustments, and you may have too much ease allowance in the circumference. Keep adjusting until you are satisfied with the pattern's fit.

- Round off the outer corners of the lining pieces near the handle bases using a tumbler as a guide.

METHOD FOR CUTTING AND SEWING

- Cut out two pattern pieces from quilter's wadding for each flap. Mark the shape of the pattern four times onto the flap fabric; two will be embroidered, two will be on the underside of the flaps. You will cut these out later after embroidery is complete.

- Trace off the basket flap embroidery pattern using a lead pencil.

- Embroider the flap tops using single-thread French knots for the berries, stem stitch for the stems, and large, single, chain stitches for the leaves. When complete, cut out around the pattern lines, being sure that a 1 cm ($^3/_8$") of seam allowance has been added.

- Place a cut layer of batting on either side of each flap, and hand sew the edges of the batting together, thus enclosing each of the cane flaps in a fixed cover of batting.

- Cut one inner base piece from lining fabric and one from quilter's batting.

- Cut four pieces of basket wall lining from lining fabric. (If pretty fabrics are in short supply, cut two of these pieces from plain, inexpensive fabric as they will not be seen underneath the upper, pretty fabric.)

- Have purchased bias piping, or some you have made yourself, sufficient to trim the perimeter of the inner basket base and around all the exposed edges of two lining pieces. Apply piping around the inner base piece and the three exposed edges of two lining pieces. To do this, place the piping and the fabric right sides facing and raw edges matching; stitch with the zipper foot of your machine. Clip the piping's seam allowance at corners for ease.

- Place the piped lining pieces together with an untrimmed lining piece and stitch around the three trimmed sides, using the previous row of stitching as a guide; again, use your zipper foot. Clip curved corners for ease, turn to right side and press.

- Baste the batting piece to the wrong side of the piped inner base piece. Mark a crease through the middle of the base piece. Gather up the unpiped edges of the lining pieces and pin each gathered edge to half of the base piece, having right sides facing and raw edges matching. The piped edges should butt together at the half-way creases. Stitch, following the stitching line for the piping.

- Place the lining fabric flap pieces over the embroidered pieces, right sides facing and raw edges even. Pin, then stitch around the curved edge, leaving the straight edge open. Turn out to the right side and slide in the batting-enclosed cane flaps.

- After adjusting the fabric cover, hand sew the open edge closed, turning in the seam allowances of the fabric pieces 1 cm ($^3/_8$").

- Push the lining and base down into the basket and adjust. Replace the covered flaps and mark with pins where holding ties can be attached to hold the flaps

Detail of basket

Lined
embroidered basket

Candlewicked bear

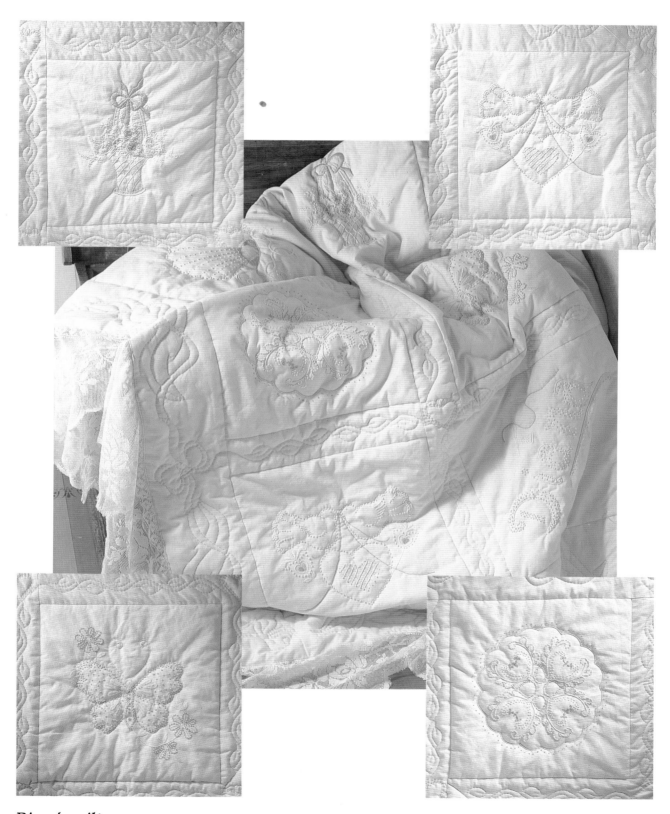

Diana's quilt

Insets: Selected details from Diana's quilt

Kirsten's quilt

Sylvia's coathanger

Sylvia's tea cosy

Detail of lid

Dianne's candlewicked box

Candlewicked cushions, edged with hand-crocheted lace

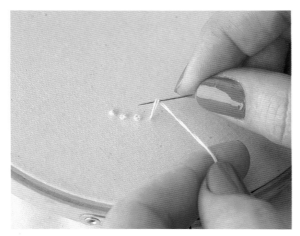

Colonial Knot — Step 1

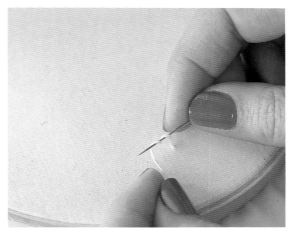

French Knot — Step 1

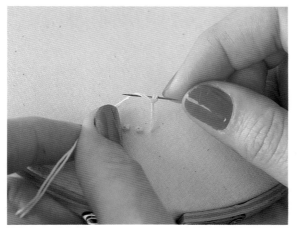

Colonial Knot — Step 2

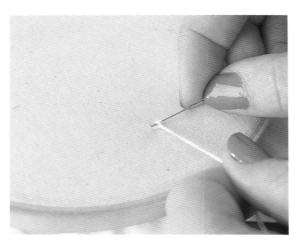

French Knot — Step 2

Colonial Knot — Step 3

in place, either around the handle bases or onto the bar across the middle of the basket.

- Make piping ties from bias strips of lining or plain fabric and attach these at the pinned marks with strong hand sewing. Tie your basket lining and flaps into position to complete.

Sewing basket courtesy of Anne d'Cavalho

The trail of berries from the top of the work basket. The stems are all stem stitch and the leaves are a single chain or lazy-daisy stitch. The dark dots should be stitched in green knots and the berries should be darker pink fading to paler pink knots

A quilt motif. The tulips, centre motif and hearts are all knots, with stem stitch for the stems and leaves. Try using thicker threads for the hearts and centre motif to give more texture

While this quilt motif is shown as all solid lines, you may like to make some areas knots and others satin stitch. Bunching knots into clusters can be an effective way to fill in areas

Sole

Ear

Head Side

Candlewicked Bear

This is a very easy bear to make because his head and body are all in one. Limbs are all sewn in rather than jointed. You can allow your creative spirit free rein when embroidering — all sorts of candlewicking embellishment will be suitable. I suggest that it would be almost impossible to embroider him too much! I've made mine from a seeded calico or muslin, although bears of other plain colours would be equally handsome.

MATERIALS

- 60 cm (24") of main fabric
- Candlewick embroidery thread
- Button eyes (optional)
- Polyester fibre stuffing

METHOD

Tip: Stitch curves twice for strength and clip into corners and around curves for ease.

- Cut out pattern pieces in numbers as directed on the pattern — 6 mm (¹/₄") seams are allowed.
- Stitch the darts in the ears, the back and front heads, the legs and the arms.
- Place the ears together in pairs and stitch around curved edge. Turn and press.
- Place legs together in pairs; leaving sole open, stitch up front and up back seams of legs, leaving an opening in the back for stuffing, and leaving open the top edges.

- Clip around the sole edge of the foot to a depth just short of 6 mm ($^1/_4$"), and pin, then stitch, the sole to this edge, right sides facing and raw edges matching. Fan out the seam allowance of the leg to make this easier. Turn legs to right side.

- Place the arms together in pairs and stitch around, leaving open the top straight edges and an opening in the back of the arm for stuffing. Turn to right side.

- Place the front and back bodies together in pairs and stitch down centre back and centre front, leaving an opening in the centre back for stuffing.

- Flatten the arms and the legs so that the seams align at the centre. The darts in the arms and legs should now be on the outside edge. Pin the arms and legs into position on the front piece as marked on the pattern. Fold the arms and legs into the centre of the body and pin to keep them out of the way of machine stitching.

- Pin the ears to the front head, aligning the darts in the ears with darts in the upper head.

- Place the body back over the body front, right sides facing and raw edges matching and pin into place. Stitch around the body. Turn the bear out through the opening in the body back.

- Stuff the legs, the arms and then the body with polyester fibre. Close the openings using ladder stitch and double thread. To avoid tangles in your sewing thread, place the end of the thread that comes off the reel first into your needle first, then knot the ends.

- Embroider your bear using knots and stem stitch around the soles, ears, body, paws and face. Stitch in your bear's nose, eyes and smile using satin stitch for the nose and chain stitch for the smile. Make three long 'lashes' fan out from each eye with simple straight stitch. Add button eyes if desired. (These must be attached very securely if a child has the bear as a toy.)

Body

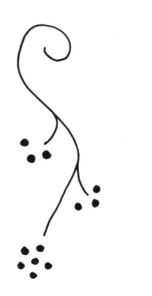

Arm

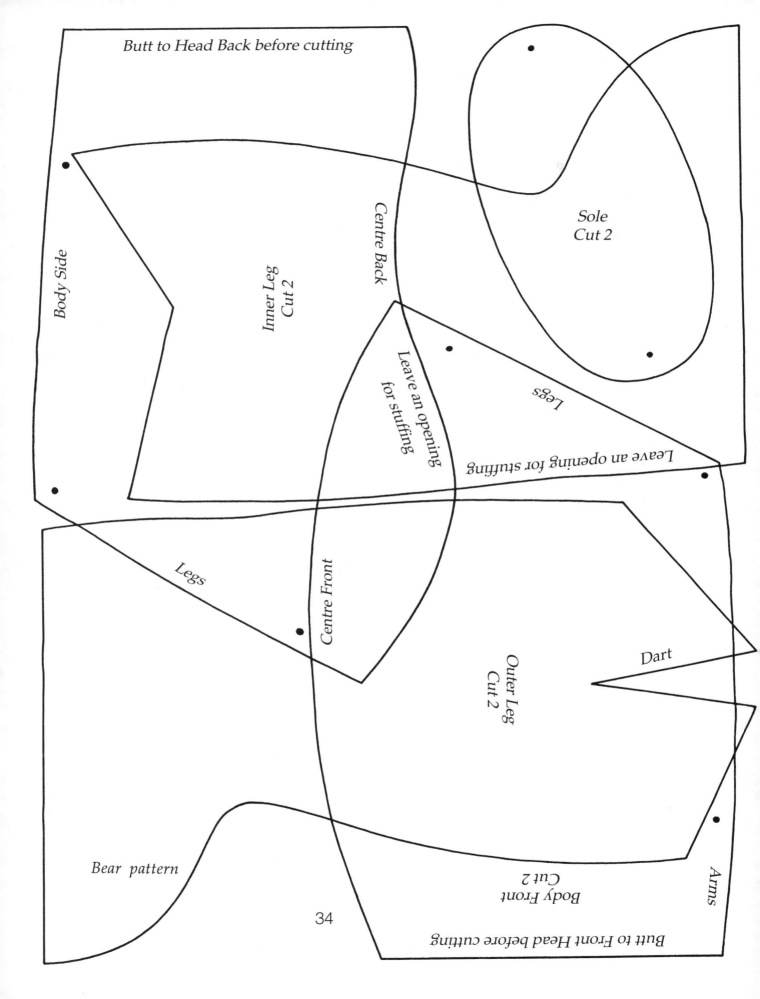

Butt to Head Back before cutting

Body Side

Centre Back

Inner Leg
Cut 2

Sole
Cut 2

Leave an opening
for stuffing

Leave an opening for stuffing

Legs

Legs

Centre Front

Dart

Outer Leg
Cut 2

Bear pattern

34

Body Front
Cut 2

Arms

Butt to Front Head before cutting

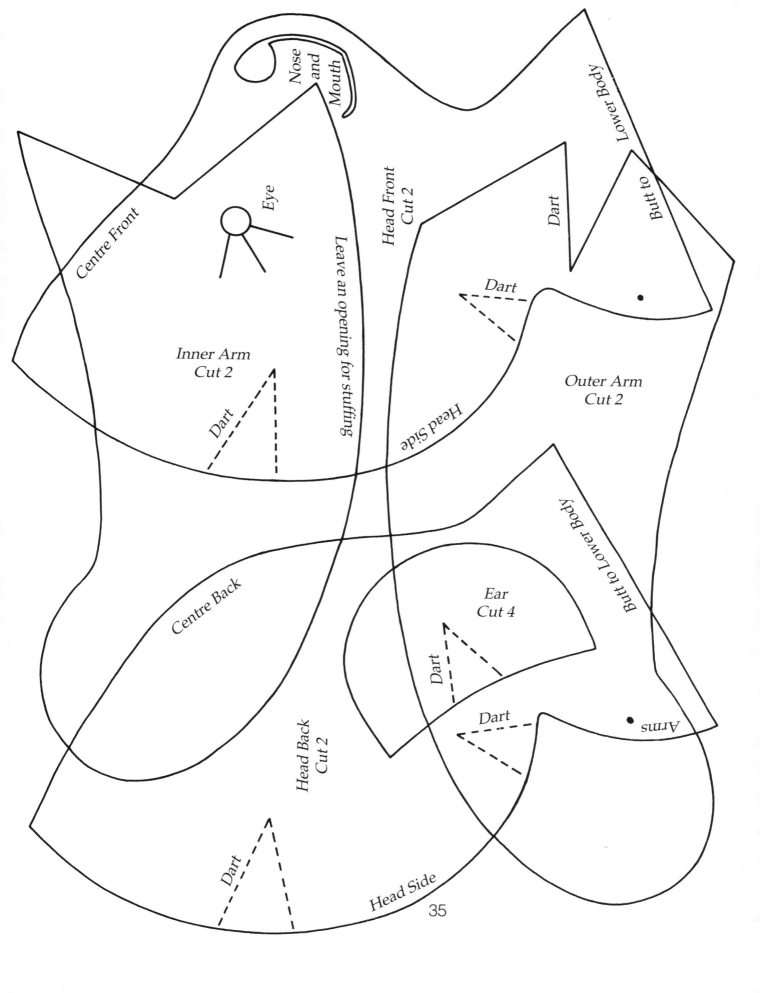

Two Heirloom Quilts

These exquisite quilts were made by two expert needlewomen as part of their major works for their final needlework diplomas. Each quilt is worked in a variety of stitches and yarns and although each quilt is very similar in its construction, the two appear quite different when finished. The following notes will help you on your way.

The construction techniques given are quite general. You may choose to change designs and stitches and add or subtract squares to produce a quilt the size you desire. In short, these ideas are meant to be inspirational, rather than precise formulae.

Both quilts are made from unbleached calico, homespun or quilter's muslin, and both are composed of squares stitched individually before the quilt is assembled.

- The illustrations of the embroidery patterns can be increased or decreased by photocopying them to a size suitable for your squares. The designs are first centred behind the squares of fabric and are then transferred to the fabric using a soft lead pencil.

- To centre a design, first be sure it sits straight on the paper. Fold the paper in half, then half again to produce the centre point. Crease the fabric square with your thumb in the same way to mark the centre. With the design behind the fabric, align the two centre points and the creases. Pin the layers together. Hold the fabric and paper against a window and trace off the pattern.

Diana's Quilt

In her wonderful quilt, Diana Clarke has used an off-white seeded calico or muslin, with a pale all-over, small print fabric for its backing. She has used assorted warm honey-coloured threads — DMC Perle No. 3 and DMC apricot stranded cotton no. 402 — to highlight and detail the designs.

The quilt fits the top of a standard double bed with a little overhang at the sides, and comprises 12 embroidered blocks that are 37 cm ($14\,^1/_2$") square finished size, each separated by tramming strips (a traditional quilting name for border strips) that are 7 cm (3") wide. The outer border is also 7 cm (3") wide. As with all quilts, a uniform amount of seam allowance should be added to each piece, usually 6 mm - 1 cm ($^1/_4$" to $^1/_2$"). Diana's long-treasured cream rose patterned lace was originally her grandmother's. It makes an exquisite finish around the sides and bottom end of the quilt.

The quilting in the tramming strips echoes the overall effect of the quilt, and is a repeat of a bow, ribbon and leaf motif. You could also extract some design feature from one of the blocks, or from the lace trimming and use this as a quilting motif.

- Once the blocks are assembled three across and four down, with tramming strips between and with the outer border in place, the quilt is ready to be hand quilted.

- Place a layer of quilter's batting between the quilt top and the backing fabric and secure these three layers together with rows of basting that fan out from the centre to each edge. It sometimes helps to hold the layers together smoothly first with large safety pins. Quilt the tramming strips with small running stitches along the drawn-in design while using a hoop. The quilted trammings give a lovely raised, textured effect to the quilt borders and give the quilt even more heirloom value.

Diana felt that her use of a variety of stitches and threads in her designs helped to highlight and define the traditional knotted stitches. She used a hoop large enough to hold the whole design, rather than have already-made stitches flattened by a smaller hoop during the embroidery process. Her designs are based on traditional candlewick motifs and abstract design adaptations. One special square is personalised with her name and some needlework motifs.

Quilt motifs. Both are shown in solid lines but lend themselves to all knots, or a combination of stem stitch and knots. Perhaps some areas could be filled in with knots

38

Quilt motif. Stem stitch, or more textured border stitches, are effective in this motif. Try adding a little colour to the butterfly if you wish. It lends itself well to sections of colour

Kirsten's Quilt

Kirsten Kreutzfeldt's beautiful lap-sized quilt would be perfect for a sofa throw-over or as an exquisite finish to a young lady's bed. This quilt is made up of 12 x 30 cm (12") square blocks, plus a uniform seam allowance, and fabric borders at the outer edges. There is no tramming, although the 6-8 cm (2$^1/_2$ - 3") wide crocheted lace stitched between the blocks gives the impression of tramming strips. A wider matching lace, about 8 - 9 cms (3 - 3$^1/_2$") is placed around the edges over the fabric border.

The fabric is unbleached, unwashed homespun or calico. Kirsten has used only cream candlewicking yarn. She has achieved very effective texture in her embroidery with the different number of threads used in knots and other stitches.

- Enlarge the designs you wish to use with a photo-copy machine. Then, transfer the design onto the centre of the fabric block using a water-soluble pen. With the block in a hoop, embroider the design using Colonial knots and stem stitch.

- Rinse the finished blocks in cold water to remove any residual ink. When dry, iron with the right side down into a fluffy towel, to avoid flattening the knots. Arrange the blocks in any order you please, positioning them three across and four down; stitch them together to make your quilt top.

- Bearing the width of your widest lace in mind, cut fabric borders for the outer edge of the quilt. When lace is added to the top of the borders, the lace will cover the border seam and sit about 2 cm (1") in from the outer edges. Stitch these across the top and bottom of the quilt, then down the sides. Open them out and press lightly.

- Place your quilter's wadding on a large flat surface, then top this with your backing fabric, right side up. Place the quilt top down onto this, wrong side up. Pin through all layers, then cut around the quilt top, neatening wadding and backing fabric edges to be level with quilt top edges. Pin around the edges. Stitch around edges, leaving an opening for turning. Turn, press lightly on the back and hand sew the opening closed.

- On the front, lay strips of narrow lace down the quilt over the two centre vertical seams so that the ends sit just on the borders. Stitch these in place, using either straight stitch, or, as Kirsten has, a wide machine wave stitch that complements the lace pattern. Stitch three narrow lace strips across the quilt, covering the seam lines; again, cut the ends to sit just on the borders.

- Stitch the wider lace across the upper and lower borders, stopping and starting just over the border seam and covering the ends of the vertical strips of narrow lace.

- Stitch the remaining wider lace down the side borders, covering the ends of the horizontal strips of narrow lace and the ends of the vertical border lace strips. Finish the ends of these strips by tucking the lace over to the back and neatening. Alternatively, undo the outside edge seam and tuck the lace ends into the cavity; re-stitch this closed by hand.

Quilt motif. Shown in solid lines, and you will have to duplicate the identical remaining side of the design. Try combinations of knots with border stitches

Sylvia's Coathanger

I believe the often-quoted expression that no woman can be too rich or too thin should be amended to add, 'or have too many padded coathangers'. They're simple to make, enduring and absolutely practical. This particular coathanger was made by Sylvia Kennedy, a noted Sydney-based teacher of embroidery and patchwork, who has a particular liking for candlewicking. I suggest you get busy and before too long you'll have enough coathangers to give away in generous bundles as very welcome presents!

MATERIALS

- 20 cm (8") cream calico or homespun

- 1 skein DMC Perle 5 (cream)

- DMC stranded cotton (cream)

- 1 wooden coathanger with metal hook

- Strips of polyester or wool wadding for padding coathanger

- Small quantity of polyester fibre stuffing for extra filling

- 25 cm (10") each of two ribbons for bows

- 15 cm (6") of cream or white satin bias binding for covering metal hook

- 1 m (40") of cream or white satin-covered piping

- Thread to match

METHOD

1 cm ($^3/_8$") seams allowed on fabric pieces.

- Trace the pattern shape of the front piece, draw on the embroidery pattern and secure the area to be embroidered in your hoop. Stitch the embroidery as follows.

44

Flowers and stems: Outline in French knots using Perle 5 single strand.

Veins and leaves: Small stem stitch using Perle 5 single strand.

Flower centres: One large French knot surrounded by small French knots, with small straight stitches fanning out from centre beyond knots.

- Cut out embroidered panel. Cut out the back and two identical lining pieces. Pin a lining piece to the back of the front, and the remaining lining piece behind the back piece. Treat them as one layer of fabric from now on.

- Starting at centre top just to one side of the hanger position, commence pinning piping around edges of front, matching raw edges and having right sides facing. Finish off piping just on remaining side of hanger position. (This leaves a gap for hanger hook.) Clip piping seam allowance at corners for ease. Using the zipper foot of your machine, stitch on piping.

- Place back and front together, right sides facing and raw edges matching. Stitch around the hanger, starting 1.5 cm ($^5/_8$") in from corner on lower edge and finishing the same distance just around the opposite corner. This leaves the base open for hanger insertion. Turn cover right side out.

- Pad hanger by wrapping batting strips around it, making sure that ends are well padded. Where necessary, use small hand stitches to hold strips in place.

- Cut satin binding to fit hook. Turn under one short end of binding and fold binding in half lengthways, wrong sides facing. Make tiny hand stitches over short end and sides to hold binding on hook. Slip binding over hook.

- Pull cover over hook and over ends of hanger. Pad cover with extra portions of polyester fibre stuffing to make sure the cover is firm and smooth.

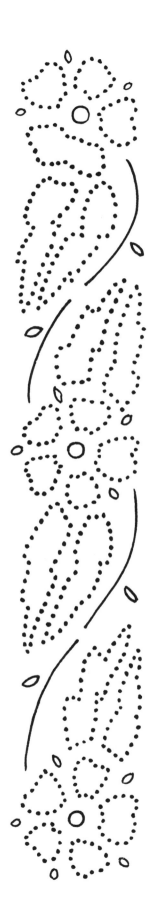

- Stitch top of cover around the base of the satin hook cover. Fold in the raw edge of the back and stitch it to the piping stitching on the front to close the lower opening.

- Tie bows around base of hook to finish.

Sylvia's Tea Cosy

Coathanger. Cut 2 of main fabric and 2 of lining.
Place on fold before cutting. The coathanger could not be more simple. The flower is in knots, the stem and leaves are worked in stem stitch.
(See pattern opposite page)

This is certainly a tea cosy with a difference. Sylvia's delightful design allows the pot to sit 'in' the cosy. The sides of the cosy are held together around the pot with ribbon bows. Quilted fabric is the key to retaining the warmth in the tea. Here, the actual candlewick stitches embellish the quilting on one side of the cosy. Read the last part of the instructions and check your tea-pot for the positions of the ties. You may find you will need to alter their position of 10 cms (3 $^1/_2$") up from the base.

Tea cosy. Cut 2 of main fabric and 2 of lining. For the base, cut 1 of main fabric and 1 of lining. Place on fold before cutting. The instructions for making the tea cosy give you details about the quilting that is combined with the stitching of its design. Knots and stem stitch are the main stitches used, with texture being added by isolated quilting around areas of the motif.
(See pattern opposite page)

MATERIALS

- 1 cm ($^3/_8$") seams allowed on fabric pieces
- 60 cm (24") cream unbleached calico or homespun
- Perle 5 thread in cream
- Stranded cotton in cream
- 30 cm (12") polyester quilter's batting
- 1.1 m (43") 2.5 cm wide (1") ribbon for ties
- 1.2 m (48") 5 cm (2") wide pre-gathered crocheted cotton lace
- Cream quilting cotton
- Matching sewing thread

47

METHOD

- Mark out two fronts (leave excess fabric around these to allow for securing in hoop), two backs and two base pieces onto fabric. Draw embroidery design on one front.

- Cut out pieces as marked, cutting excess fabric around fronts. Cut out one back and one base from quilter's batting. Cut out a batting piece slightly larger than the fronts.

- Place plain back down on flat surface, place batting piece on top, then the remaining back piece. Repeat this with the base pieces. Pin, then baste the various layers together.

- Mark out a criss-cross grid on one side of the back and base pieces. This can be simply done if your machine has a quilting guide — an extension 'arm' that attaches to your machine foot and allows you to make successive rows of stitching an even distance apart. If you don't have this gadget, mark in evenly spaced lines using a lead pencil or dressmaker's chalk. Stitch along these lines to quilt the pieces.

- Layer with batting and baste the front pieces as you did for the backs and base, having the patterned piece facing upwards. You have excess fabric and batting around the edge of the pattern piece to make working with a hoop easier. Secure the piece in your hoop and quilt around the embroidery pattern, taking tiny running stitches through the layers and pulling your thread firmly to emphasise the design. I suggest you use double thread in your needle to quilt.

- Following the guide below, make the stitches in the quilting indentations.

  Tulips: Using Perle 5 doubled, make the flower outline in French knots. Using Perle 5 single strand, back stitch top of tulip.
  Leaves: Using Perle 5 doubled, outline in French knots. Using Perle 5 single strand, back stitch veins.
  Stems: Using two strands of stranded cotton make the stems in stem stitch.

- When embroidery is complete, cut the front piece out accurately using pattern piece, being sure to centre the embroidery.

- Pin lace around curved edges of front and back, having right sides facing and lower edge of lace even with edges of front and back. Stitch lace into place.

- Cut ribbon into four equal sections and pin each piece 10 cm (3 $1/2$") up from the base on the curved edge of the front and back, so that there are two each on the front and back. These are the ties that hold the cosy around the pot. The short end of the ribbon should be even with the seam allowances; ribbon should be laying across right sides of front and back.

- Cut bias strips of fabric from scraps (piece these together if necessary to make up 1.20 m (48") length) 2 cm (1") wide. Press these in half lengthways to have raw edges even.

- Pin, then stitch, raw edge of binding around curved edges of front and back, on top of the lace, stretching it slightly around the curve.

- Trim back raw edges close to stitching. Fold bias back to inside and slip stitch folded edge to previous machine stitching.

- Fold base in half and pin edges at fold line. Fold back and front in half to find centre of each piece. Align pins and pin back and front around base, folding lace of back piece inside at lower edge. Stitch around circle, trim back seam allowance and overcast raw edges.

- To use, insert the tea-pot in the cosy and tie bows above the spout and through the handle. This style of cosy would work equally well for a coffee pot — you could tailor the two sides of the cosy to any dimensions to fit your pot.

49

Dianne's Candlewicked Box

If you're a beginner, let this box be an inspiration to you. My good friend, Di Skarratt, had not done any candlewicking until I asked her to work this box for me. The beautiful results should be an inspiration to anyone! And, I should add that Di is now contemplating the design of her next candlewick project — probably a quilt. The top panel had started out as a cushion top, until I thought that an embroidered box might look rather fetching. The top and sides are worked before the box is covered, and, given that there are boxes of many shapes and sizes, this project must serve as an inspiration, rather than a precise pattern. The French knots were worked with three strands of candlewicking yarn. The satin and chain stitches were worked with two strands. The narrow crocheted lace trim is optional, but it does serve to cover join lines and adds its own pretty touch.

Traditionally, boxes are first covered with a layer of thin-to medium-thickness, polyester fibre quilter's batting, which is held in place by gluing the appropriate-sized panels to the various surfaces of the box. The outer fabric layer is usually glued or stitched into place over this batting, all the while allowing for any closures and avoiding unwanted thickness where the lid might slide down over the base. Every box has its own needs as far as shapes are concerned, and it's seldom a uniform process to cover a box with fabric. However, the following instructions will give you some idea of how to cover a round, lidded box inside and out.

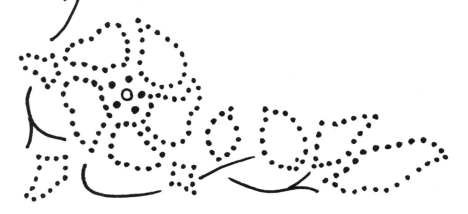

MATERIALS

- Fabric for box sides, top and base, inside and out

- Batting to cover every surface of box, except inside lid and box sides

- Embroidery thread as required

- Matching sewing thread

- Lace trim (optional)

- Glue, such as white PVA, or clear lampshade maker's glue

METHOD

- Make paper patterns of the various surfaces of your box and label them. All visible edges on the finished box have had their raw edges folded under. Allow 1 cm ($^3/_8$") seam allowances or fold-unders and remember that these pieces will need to go over the thickness of your batting.

- The outer side pieces of the lid and box should be cut to extend over the lip of the box or lid and down into it to rest on the base.

- Cut these pieces from unbleached calico or homespun if they are not to be embroidered. Draw out the pieces to be embroidered onto your fabric. Add your embroidery pattern with a lead pencil or a water-soluble pen, spacing the motifs evenly as desired. Work the embroidery using a hoop to hold the fabric taut. When embroidery is complete, wash and dry the fabric. Press lightly on the wrong side, then cut out the pieces.

- Glue batting over all surfaces of the box, except the inner lid and box sides, and on the outside where the lid slides over the top of the box. Cut a batting piece to fit the inner base, but do not glue it into place yet. Do not overlap the batting, rather trim it to butt together at meeting points. I sometimes like to stitch it together to hold it at tricky points. Glue is applied with a paintbrush, or in lines squeezed from the bottle, whichever is appropriate.

- Lay on the box base piece and bring its allowances up onto the sides of the box. Baste them in place to the batting. Fold over the edges of the side panels and take this around the box, overlapping the short edges. Keep the lower folded edge right on the lower edge of the box, covering the base allowance. Pin to secure.

- Fold the remaining fabric down into the box and adjust. Stitch or glue this in place, being sure that the fabric is taut, the embroidery is evenly placed and the edges of the base piece are securely held. I like to stitch the lower edge of the box side piece to the base piece. It's worth noting that this step can take a fair amount of fiddling and fixing — so be patient and you'll achieve wonderful results.

- Cover the inside base wadding piece with the fabric, tucking it under and basting it around the edges to hold. Glue it down into the base, removing the basting before the glue is dry. If your edge here is unsatisfactory, you may wish to tuck it in and glue some lace around base to disguise it.

- Cover the lid of the box in much the same way as you covered the base; it helps if you regard it as a shallow box and treat it exactly as you treated the box itself, except that the top of the lid is padded. Be sure to centre the embroidery evenly on the top. Stitch or glue some lace around the lid edge if desired.

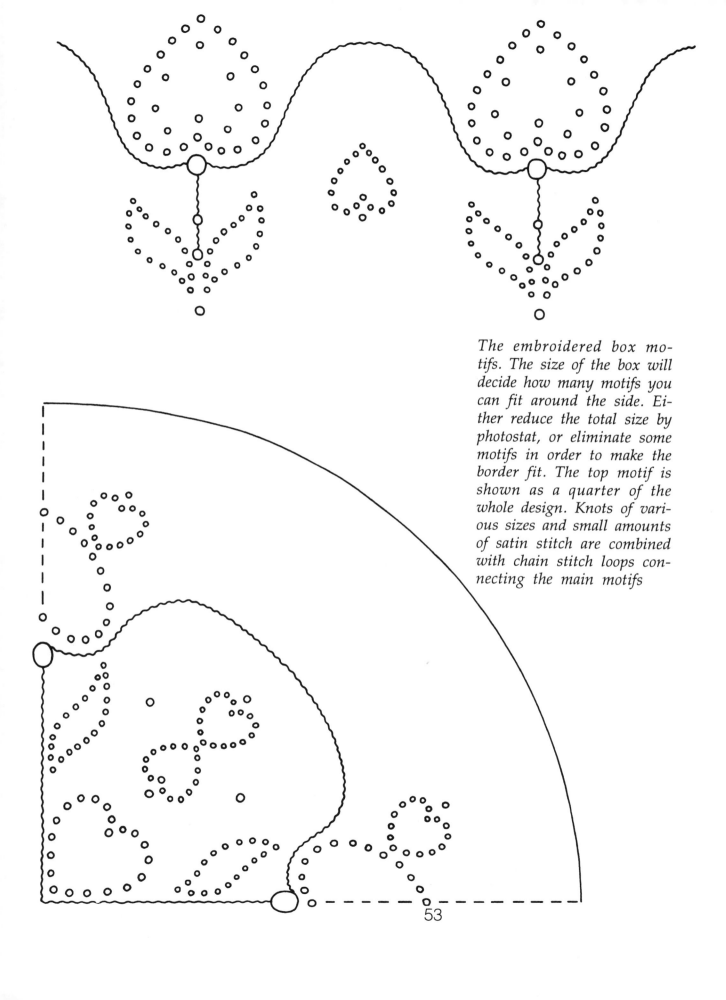

The embroidered box motifs. The size of the box will decide how many motifs you can fit around the side. Either reduce the total size by photostat, or eliminate some motifs in order to make the border fit. The top motif is shown as a quarter of the whole design. Knots of various sizes and small amounts of satin stitch are combined with chain stitch loops connecting the main motifs

53

Two Pretty Cushions

Cushion tops give you tremendous scope for displaying candlewick embroidery. The traditional designs used in those pictured are just a few small examples of what is possible with cushions. So let your imagination go when deciding on your pattern.

The perfect partner for candlewicking seems to be cream crocheted lace, and I use it whenever possible. Most square cushions are around 40 cm (16") square. There seems to be a good supply of commercially made cushion inserts for cushions of this size.

The embroidery worked here was made with candlewick thread, using two or three strands in the French knots. Transfer the design onto the cushion front using a lead pencil or a soluble pen.

A cushion front design. All the dots are knots, the stems and centre rails are in stem stitch. The leaves could be in stem stitch but also lend themselves to a more textured border stitch

54

A cushion front design. All the dots are knots, with thicker-than-usual thread being used for more texture

55

MATERIALS

- Embroidered front for your cushion front and a plain back, cut to the same size

- Lace for edge. (Read Method section following before purchasing)

- Cushion insert

- Sewing thread

METHOD

- The lace is overlapped at the corners and then stitched through to mitre the corner. The excess lace is cut away from the front and back leaving only the width of the satin stitch seam. Note the illustration for the positioning of the lace strips and allow sufficient extra lace at each corner to stitch the lace in this way. The extra amount for the corners will depend on the width of your lace.

- Place the front and back cushion pieces together, right sides facing and raw edges even. Stitch around leaving a 30 cm (12") opening on one side for stuffing. Trim corners of bulk and turn to right side. Press the edges, making sure the seam line is even.

- Lay the lace along the pressed edges, overlapping the corners as shown. Turn your machine to a stitch that stitches straight and has a regular zig-zag stitch in its sequence. Place the straight stitch close to the edge of the cushion and the zig-zag will move across and fasten the edge of the lace. If you do not have this stitch, use all zig-zag, or some other similar stitch, making it as narrow as you need in order to fasten the lace to the cushion edges.

- When the lace edges are fastened, pin the corners into place and turn your machine to a medium zig-zag. Stitch from the cushion corner diagonally out to the edges of the lace.

- Cut away the excess lace from the top and below the seam, leaving only the seam line. Take care doing this and be sure you don't cut away the wrong layer — it would be disastrous! Turn your machine to a closer zig-zag stitch and stitch again over the previous stitching, enclosing the raw edges.

- Insert the cushion insert and hand sew the opening closed.

Quilt motif. Shown in solid lines, and you will have to duplicate the identical remaining side of the design. Try combinations of knots with border stitches

Other Books in the Milner Craft Series

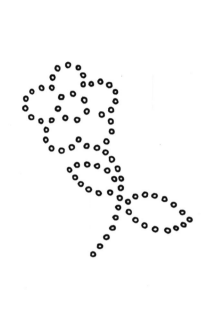